30 DAY MASTERY
SPOKEN
JAPANESE
MADE SIMPLE

Master Natural, Conversational Japanese in 30 Days

by Olly Richards

Edited by Eleonora Calviello & Leonardo Vinueza

Jeremy Rasmussen, Language Consultant

Copyright © 2022 Olly Richards Publishing Ltd.

All rights reserved. No part of this publication may be reproduced, distributed or transmitted in any form or by any means, including photocopying, recording, or other electronic or mechanical methods, without the prior written permission of the publisher, except in the case of brief quotations embodied in critical reviews and certain other non-commercial uses permitted by copyright law. For permission requests, write to the publisher:

Olly Richards Publishing Ltd.

olly@storylearning.com

Trademarked names appear throughout this book. Rather than use a trademark symbol with every occurrence of a trademarked name, names are used in an editorial fashion, with no intention of infringement of the respective owner's trademark.

The information in this book is distributed on an "as is" basis, without warranty. Although every precaution has been taken in the preparation of this work, neither the author nor the publisher shall have any liability to any person or entity with respect to any loss or damage caused or alleged to be caused directly or indirectly by the information contained in this book.

30 Day Mastery Spoken Japanese Made Simple: Master Natural, Conversational Japanese in 30 Days

FREE STORYLEARNING® KIT

Discover how to learn foreign languages faster & more effectively through the power of story.

Your free video masterclasses, action guides & handy printouts include:

- A simple six-step process to maximise learning from reading in a foreign language

- How to double your memory for new vocabulary from stories

- Planning worksheet (printable) to learn faster by reading more consistently

- Listening skills masterclass: "How to effortlessly understand audio from stories"

- How to find willing native speakers to practise your language with

To claim your FREE StoryLearning® Kit, visit:

www.storylearning.com/kit

WE DESIGN OUR BOOKS TO BE INSTAGRAMMABLE!

Post a photo of your new book to Instagram using #storylearning and you'll get an entry into our monthly book giveaways!

Tag us **@storylearningpress** to make sure we see you!

BOOKS BY OLLY RICHARDS

Olly Richards writes books to help you learn languages through the power of story. Here is a list of all currently available titles:

Short Stories in Danish For Beginners
Short Stories in Dutch For Beginners
Short Stories in English For Beginners
Short Stories in French For Beginners
Short Stories in German For Beginners
Short Stories in Icelandic For Beginners
Short Stories in Italian For Beginners
Short Stories in Norwegian For Beginners
Short Stories in Brazilian Portuguese For Beginners
Short Stories in Russian For Beginners
Short Stories in Spanish For Beginners
Short Stories in Swedish For Beginners
Short Stories in Turkish For Beginners

Short Stories in Arabic for Intermediate Learners
Short Stories in English for Intermediate Learners
Short Stories in Italian for Intermediate Learners

Short Stories in Korean for Intermediate Learners
Short Stories in Spanish for Intermediate Learners

101 Conversations in Simple English
101 Conversations in Simple French
101 Conversations in Simple German
101 Conversations in Simple Italian
101 Conversations in Simple Spanish

101 Conversations in Intermediate English
101 Conversations in Intermediate French
101 Conversations in Intermediate German
101 Conversations in Intermediate Italian
101 Conversations in Intermediate Spanish

101 Conversations in Mexican Spanish
101 Conversations in Social Media Spanish
Climate Change in Simple Spanish
World War II in Simple Spanish

All titles are also available as audiobooks. Just search your favourite store!

For more information visit Olly's author page at:
www.storylearning.com/books

ABOUT THE AUTHOR

Olly Richards is a foreign language expert and teacher. He speaks eight languages and has authored over 30 books. He has appeared in international press, from the BBC and the Independent to El País and Gulf News. He has featured in language documentaries and authored language courses for the Open University.

Olly started learning his first foreign language at the age of 19, when he bought a one-way ticket to Paris. With no exposure to languages growing up, and no natural talent for languages, Olly had to figure out how to learn French from scratch. Twenty years later, Olly has studied languages from around the world and is considered an expert in the field.

Through his books and website, StoryLearning.com, Olly is known for teaching languages through the power of story – including the book you are holding in your hands right now!

You can find out more about Olly, including a library of free training, at his website:

www.storylearning.com

CONTENTS

ABOUT THIS SERIES xv

HOW 30-DAY MASTERY WORKS xvii

THE 6-STEP READING PROCESS xxi

LANGUAGE OVERVIEW: 7 THINGS TO KNOW
TO UNDERSTAND SPOKEN JAPANESE xxiv

INTRODUCTION TO THE STORY 3

第一章：小林家族 4
Quiz: Day 1 6

第二章：忙しい朝 10
Quiz: Day 2 12

第三章：アレックス の高校 16
Quiz: Day 3 18

第四章：スーパー 22
Quiz: Day 4 24

第五章：久のカフェ 28
Quiz: Day 5 30

第六章：祖父母の銭湯 34
Quiz: Day 6 36

第七章：お盆休み 40
Quiz: Day 7 42

第八章：旅行の準備	46
Quiz: Day 8	48
第九章：出発	52
Quiz: Day 9	54
第十章：京都	58
Quiz: Day 10	60
第十一章：芸者さん	64
Quiz: Day 11	66
第十二章：お寺	70
Quiz: Day 12	72
第十三章：五山送り火	76
Quiz: Day 13	78
第十四章：京都最終日	82
Quiz: Day 14	84
第十五章：兵庫県	88
Quiz: Day 15	90
第十六章：城崎温泉	94
Quiz: Day 16	96
第十七章：城崎温泉の夜	100
Quiz: Day 17	102
第十八章：初めての飛行機	106
Quiz: Day 18	108
第十九章：札幌	112
Quiz: Day 19	114

第二十章：湯の川温泉	118
Quiz: Day 20	120
第二十一章：函館観光	124
Quiz: Day 21	126
第二十二章：函館の夜景	130
Quiz: Day 22	132
第二十三章：サル山温泉	136
Quiz: Day 23	138
第二十四章：函館港まつり	142
Quiz: Day 24	144
第二十五章：屋台	148
Quiz: Day 25	150
第二十六章：花火	154
Quiz: Day 26	156
第二十七章：登別温泉	158
Quiz: Day 27	160
第二十八章：富良野	164
Quiz: Day 28	166
第二十九章：札幌	170
Quiz: Day 29	172
第三十章：小林家の未来	176
Quiz: Day 30	178
Answer Key	185
Notes	193

ABOUT THIS SERIES

Dear Language Learner,

This series offers you the chance to learn difficult things a little more easily. If you've ever tried learning a language from a textbook or in a traditional classroom but found that things just didn't "click", this series is for you.

Here's the big idea: You've tried learning through rules, lectures, textbooks, and tests, but it didn't work (or it only half-worked, leaving you confused and frustrated). Traditional language learning works on this idea: "Just learn the rules, then you'll know the language!" But you soon discover that a rules-based approach to language learning only gets you so far.

Here, you're going to learn through an exciting new method called StoryLearning®. The StoryLearning® method helps you learn languages quickly – through stories, not rules. It uses the same natural learning process children use to learn their native language.

Every book in this series focuses on a different area of language. For the most part, it's grammar, but we also venture into other difficult areas, such as idioms and writing systems. The concept of the books is that you immerse yourself fully in one difficult area of language for 30 days. Smart language learners know that it takes time to learn difficult concepts. With 30 days of focus with StoryLearning®, you can learn more than you might in years of sporadic rule-based learning.

Give me your full attention for the next 30 days and you'll never go back to learning the old way again. Grammar rules that used to slip your mind will come naturally to you. Concepts that made no sense will start to "sound right". Idioms that once confused you will bring a knowing smile to your face. I've learnt eight languages using the methods in this book, and I'm excited to introduce them to you too.

Welcome to a better way to learn languages. Welcome to StoryLearning®.

Get ready for things to "click".

To your success,

Olly Richards

HOW 30-DAY MASTERY WORKS

The 30-Day Mastery series uses StoryLearning® to help you master one particular area of language. These are the so-called "tricky" areas of language, such as a difficult grammar point, confusing idioms, or unfamiliar writing systems, such as Japanese *kanji*. As the name implies, you will be focusing on this one topic for 30 days. To maximise your depth of *focus*, these 30 days should be consecutive where possible. The *consistency* will pay off!

At first glance, the book appears to be a simple story, and it is; the book is one complete story, told over 30 chapters. But there's more. Although the story stands alone as an entertaining read (*motivating*), its main purpose is to put the topic of the book in *context*. In fact, the story is jam-packed with examples of the particular language focus of the book. For example, if the topic of the book is the subjunctive, you will find examples of the subjunctive throughout the story – always natural, and always in context.

Over the 30 days of the challenge, reading one chapter of the story per day, you will be bombarded with naturally occurring examples of the language topic within the pages of the story. Your job is simply to look out for *(notice)* where and how this language is being used. Over 30 days of intense depth and focus on the main language point, your brain will gradually get used to how the topic works, in just the same way as a child picks up the correct language from their surroundings.

Built into the stories are plenty of other features to help you learn:

- A linguistic summary of the topic of the book, to ensure you are aware of the key information and rules and make sure you know what to look for as you read

- The stories are carefully written at a low-intermediate level (A2-B1, equivalent to JLPT N4 in the case of Japanese), so you can concentrate on the topic without being distracted by difficult vocabulary

- The chapters are short – around 200 words – so you can easily complete one chapter per day without it becoming overwhelming

- Bilingual word lists at the end of each chapter help you quickly look up difficult words, so you can keep reading without fumbling with a dictionary

- Simple practice exercises give you the chance to test your understanding as you go. The point is to flex your learning muscles by being active in the learning process *(deliberate practice)*, rather than just reading the story passively

- An audio edition of each book is also available, so you can listen along as you read, giving you a deeper way to consume the story and can help speed up learning

If you can commit to spending 30 days with this book, the results will be transformative. The expectation is not that you will develop complete mastery within 30 days, but rather that you develop a native-like understanding of the topic, one that you cannot get from conscious learning. With this native-like understanding, you will be better able to use language instinctively, automatically, and "without thinking" over time, and this paves the way to reaching higher levels of fluency *(understand first, speak later)*.

Just like a child's learning, the 30 days of this challenge will not be a linear process. Expect bumps along the way. You will notice the main effects of this book only when the 30 days are complete, as it is the cumulative effect of the study, not any single day's study, that delivers the transformation. As such, don't worry if there are days when nothing seems to make sense!

After helping thousands of students to reach their language goals, I have found that the most successful students are those who learn to be happy with ambiguity, and trust in the process. Your secret weapon will be *consistency*. So, come back every day and let StoryLearning® do the work!

THE 6-STEP READING PROCESS

Here is my suggested six-step process for making the most of the 30-Day Mastery series:

1. **Read the language overview.** This will make you aware of all the key facts and rules relating to the topic of the book. Don't worry about learning or memorising this information. It is intended as a signpost and meant to give you an awareness of the topic will help focus your attention as you read and engage your whole brain in the learning.

2. **Read the short plot summary at the beginning of the story.** This sets the context for the story, and will help you understand what you read.

3. **Read each chapter all the way through without stopping.** Your aim is simply to reach the end of the chapter, so don't worry if there are things you don't understand. Simply try to follow the gist of the story. If you get stuck, you can use the vocabulary list at the end of the chapter to check unknown words and phrases.

4. **Go back and read the same chapter a second time.** This time, try to actively *notice* where the language topic appears. Ask yourself questions like: "Why is this being used here?"; "What meaning does it convey?"; and "Is there a particular form or variation being used?" In the early chapters, you might like to refer back to the language overview to remind yourself of the key information. But don't slip into 'study mode' here! Your

job is to be curious, ask "Why?", and stay focused on enjoying the story.

5. **Complete the practice exercises at the end of the chapter.** These are optional, but you may find that some deliberate practice helps engage your brain and speed up learning.

6. **Come back the next day!** Remember, the value from this book comes from using it consistently over 30 days, not from intensive study of each chapter. So, once you've completed chapter one, put the book down and come back the next day. You should follow the same process every day for the remaining chapters.

Remember, StoryLearning® works gradually, not overnight. At every stage of the process, there will inevitably be words and phrases you do not understand or passages you find confusing. Instead of worrying about the things you *don't* understand, try to focus instead on everything that you *do* understand, and set your sights on completing the entire 30-day course!

Note: If you have the accompanying audiobook, you should *listen while reading* at every stage of the process. Having the audio also allows you to easily review chapters you have already studied at points during the day when reading is not practical.

LANGUAGE OVERVIEW: 7 THINGS TO KNOW TO UNDERSTAND SPOKEN JAPANESE

The first step on any language learning journey usually lands a student in the pages of a textbook, using writing-focused language practice that relies heavily on written exercises to test reading comprehension and handwriting. But as any fluent speaker will tell you, reading and writing are only a small part of truly knowing a language.

For example, you would use a different tone and vocabulary if you were speaking to a friend versus writing an email to your boss, right? You might use slang, swear, or speak in broken or informal sentences to your friend, but you wouldn't dream of doing that with your boss. Even the acts of writing and speaking are different when you consider the many ways we change how we communicate when we're speaking rather than when we're writing.

Depending on the context, the way we use language – and the language we speak – changes drastically. This is true for most languages, but it is especially true for Japanese. To develop and grow as a learner of Japanese, it's important to understand the ways the language changes depending on whether you're speaking or writing it.

Spoken Japanese and written Japanese differ in seven major areas. This can make it feel intimidating, but with a little knowledge and a lot of practice, you'll go far!

1. Homophones

Homophones are words that have the same pronunciation but different spellings and meanings, like *knew* and *new*. In English, homophones are less common than in Japanese, where they arise regularly because of the consistency and regularity of Japanese sounds. Where English has complex sounds like "sch" and "ough", which make words that resemble one another sound different (like *thought* and *though*), Japanese has a relatively small number of total sounds that are always pronounced the same way.

This means you're going to run into a lot of homophones when you're speaking Japanese. 者 and 物 (*mono*), or person vs. thing, and 早い or 速い (*hayai*), which is early vs. fast. It's easy to distinguish between the two when you can see the words written down, but you must listen closely to understand which meaning is meant in a conversation.

Imagine you're listening to someone speaking and they say the word *kanji*. If this were written Japanese, you would be able to distinguish their meaning by seeing the text: either 漢字, the Japanese characters, or 感じ, as in a feeling. They both sound exactly the same, and they're both nouns, which means your understanding rests on your ability to listen actively and use the context clues around you in real time.

2. Onomatopoeia

Another thing you'll run into when speaking Japanese are onomatopoeias, which are words that are created to convey the sound of the thing being named. In English, words like *buzz* and *zing* are onomatopoeia. Becoming familiar with some of the common onomatopoeia in Japanese will help you in conversation and boost your oral understanding.

Here are some examples of onomatopoeia in Japanese:

- ペラペラ *perapera*, speaking a foreign language fluently or well
- ごろごろ *gorogoro*, the sound of something like a boulder rolling
- もやもや *moyamoya*, worrying or being unsure

3. Formal and Informal Language

Remember the introductory paragraph's example about how you would presumably speak differently to a friend than you would when writing to your boss? Well, that example is even more true in Japanese. It is unlikely that you will encounter very casual language in written Japanese, but it's very likely that you'll hear very casually spoken Japanese.

Consider the ways we do this in English. For example, it's easy to slur together and cut-off pieces of words in the common phrase, "nah, dun rully feel likit". Even if you wrote that phrase out in a casual text, you would probably write something like, "nah, don't really feel like it". But when the phrase is spoken quickly, it sounds almost like a different language, though a fluent speaker would know exactly what you meant.

The same is true for Japanese. Though it is almost always formal when written, the spoken variant is drastically different.

For example, let's look at the phrase "what are you doing?"

Written:

なにをやっているんですか

Nani wo yatteirun desu ka?

This is a fairly average, formal sentence in written Japanese. It contains the particles *wo* and *ka*, and uses the full conjugation of *desu* instead of *da*.

Spoken:

なにやってんの

Nani yatten no?

This is a common utterance in spoken, casual Japanese and is the same sentence and meaning as the first. But notice how truncated the sentence has become: the particles are missing, the conjugation is mostly untouched, and even the question particle *ka* is left off.

In addition to using context clues and paying attention to onomatopoeia, understanding how often shorthand phrases are used in casual, "standard" spoken Japanese is critical to your growth as a speaker. These shortening methods, like using *-ssu* in place of *desu* or *suimasen* instead of *sumimasen*, are sometimes even referred to as "contractions" in Japanese.

4. Japanese Slang

Using slang and expanding your vocabulary specifically for oral use can take your fluency as a speaker to the next level. Though written slang does exist, it's much more common when spoken. Even if you're not comfortable using slang at first, it's helpful to know some of the more common phrases so you understand them if someone else uses them during a conversation!

Some phrases you'll run into are:

- やばい *yabai*, which can mean almost anything, but is mostly used as an intensifier, ranging in use from "that's awful" to "that's amazing".
- イケメン *ikemen*, which means handsome and well-groomed.
- マジで *maji de*, which means "Seriously!?" or "No way!"

5. The Influence of Dialects

Just like in the United Kingdom and the United States, Japanese can be incredibly diverse in what words are used and how they're pronounced depending on the region you're in. For example, imagine an English language learner going to the deep south of the United States and hearing words like "y'all" in a thick southern accent, or even how different English in the United Kingdom is from English in the United States. Something as small as "soda" versus "pop" can be confusing when you're learning to speak a new language.

The same is true for Japan's regions, and when you're learning Japanese. Take a deep dive into the specific slang and dialects of the areas that are of the most interest to you in Japan! You're sure to find some interesting and illuminating differences between regions.

For now, as a brief overview, know that Tokyo's dialect, Tokyo-ben, is the most common dialect used. Many of the slang words that you may pick up from anime are Tokyo-ben, which includes, for example, a word like すげ *suge*, which is an altered and casual version of *sugoi*, or "amazing".

The other most well-known dialect, Kansai-ben, is from the Kansai region of Japan. Kansai-ben speakers swap *hen* for *masen* in words, so that, for example, 分かりません *wakarimasen* (I don't know) becomes *wakarahen* instead.

6. Puns and Dad Jokes

As it turns out, dad jokes have universal appeal! In Japan, puns, or *dajare*, have spawned a subset of jokes known as *oyagi ayagu* or "middle-aged man gags". This is a kind of wordplay that you will only hear in spoken Japanese, not written, as it relies on the ambiguity and nuance of the spoken Japanese language. For example, imagine you say the following blankly and without pause:

Pansukutta

If you wrote this in Japanese characters, it would give away the gag as the meaning would be immediately clear! In spoken Japanese, this could be translated as both "I made bread" and "I ate pants", depending on when you pause within the sentence. This funny, playful language only exists in spoken Japanese, so it's worth getting familiar with a few so you're in on the joke when it comes up in conversation.

7. Filler and Pause Words

Filler and pause words are so common in spoken language that we hardly notice them in our native languages, but they are an aspect of any language that you can easily get tripped up on! In English, we use words like "uh", "um", "mmm", or "huh" to fill gaps while we're thinking or confused about something. Sometimes, those same words can express awkwardness, concern, or uncertainty when we're reacting to something someone said.

Rather than using English filler words, it's important to know the words Japanese speakers use, both to improve your own fluency and to understand the flow of conversation around you. Start using filler words as early as possible so that you can train your mind to use the ones in your new language rather than reverting to English.

Here are a few you could try:

- *Eeto* – um
- *Ano* – um, more common among women but fine for both genders
- *Ma* – well, okay
- *Ee?* – a noise of surprise; sometimes pronounced as *hee?*
- *Naruhodo* – I see; used to indicate you are listening

Be wary of the common mistake made by English speakers: combining *eeto* with the drawn-out pronunciation of *uhh* in English. It ends up sounding like "ee…", which is already a Japanese filler phrase that communicates surprise!

Don't Be Afraid of Spoken Japanese

You might be feeling a little overwhelmed by how much spoken Japanese differs from the written words you've been learning. But if you gradually incorporate learning spoken Japanese alongside the text you're used to, you'll become both a more well-rounded language learner and gain a better understanding of the nuances in the Japanese language. Don't think of spoken Japanese and written Japanese as two separate entities: they're all one, evolving form!

Immerse yourself in the language and see how far you go. Don't be afraid to make mistakes, and speak Japanese as often as you can!

温泉
レスキュー
の旅

INTRODUCTION TO THE STORY

Alex is a young exchange student who has lived in Japan for about six months with a loving foster family made up of Akemi, Hiroshi, their children, and grandparents Yoshiko and Jiro, owners of a sentou, or bathhouse.

However, when Yoshiko and Jiro's business starts to fail, Akemi and Hiroshi decide to take the whole family on a trip across Japan in order to find inspiration on how to modernise and save the bathhouse, and the family, from certain ruin.

From the geisha district in Kyoto to the hot springs of Hakodate, Alex and his new family see Japanese culture in all of its varied beauty and learn about different traditions, dialects, and cultures across the small island nation.

第一章
小林家族

42歳の明美と50歳の久は、子供が4人もいる。一番上のお姉ちゃんは16歳の玲。真ん中の弟は10歳の直人。一番下は双子で、武と瞳。まだ3歳だ。6ヶ月前アレックスという留学生が、小林一家でホームステイを始めた。近くにおじいちゃんとおばあちゃんも住んでいるので、小林家は大家族だ。小林家には犬のクロもいる。

明美は、武と瞳が寝る前、毎日本を読んであげる。

明美：そして、王子様とお姫様は、幸せに暮らしましたとさ。おしまい。

瞳：え〜、もう終わり？

武：もっと、読んで〜。次は、え〜っと・・・裸の王様がいい！

明美：もう夜9時だから、寝る時間よ。裸の王様は明日読んであげる。二人とも目をつぶって。ちゃんと布団に入りなさい。

瞳(ひとみ)＆武(たけし)：は〜い。

クロ：ワンワン！

語彙(ごい)

歳(さい) age, years old

真(ま)ん中(なか) middle, centre

一番下(いちばんした) the lowest

留学生(りゅうがくせい) overseas student, exchange student

つぶって (つぶる) shut, close one's eyes

QUIZ
DAY 1

1. How many children do Akemi and Hisashi have?

   a. 2
   b. 3
   c. 4
   d. 5

2. Who is the oldest child?

   a. Naoto
   b. Rei
   c. Hitomi
   d. Takeshi

3. How old are the twins?

   a. 1 year
   b. 2 years
   c. 3 years
   d. 4 years

4. Which of these is used to express surprise or dissatisfaction?

   a. え〜
   b. なんか
   c. じゃぁ
   d. えっと

5. Fill in the blanks to complete the conversation between A and B.

   A: 今日、何をしましたか？（きょう、なにをしましたか）
   B: ___、ジムに行って、洗濯を洗って、日本語を勉強したよ。(___, ジムにいって、せんたくをあらって、にほんごをべんきょうしたよ)

   a. え〜
   b. なんか
   c. じゃぁ
   d. えっと

6. Which of the following is used to "buy time" when speaking?

   a. え〜
   b. なんか
   c. じゃぁ
   d. えっと

7. Fill in the blanks to complete the conversation between A and B.

   A: もう、アイスはないよ。
   B: ___、残念。。。(___, ざんねん。。。)

   a. え〜
   b. なんか
   c. じゃぁ
   d. えっと

8. True or False: え〜and えっと can be used interchangeably.

   a. True
   b. False

9. True or False: Alex has been adopted by the Kobayashi family.

   a. True
   b. False

10. According to the story, what is Akemi going to do tomorrow?

    a. She is going to go shopping
    b. She is going to help Alex study Japanese
    c. She is going to a hot spring
    d. She is going to read a story to the twins

第二章
忙しい朝

朝になり、久は仕事に行く支度を始めた。子供達とアレックスも起きて、一階に下りてきた。明美は朝ご飯の支度をし、家族皆が椅子に座り、朝ご飯を食べ始めた。

明美：玲、今日部活の後、何時頃帰ってくる？

玲：う〜ん、多分・・・6時くらい。

明美：直人、帽子持っていくの忘れないでね。今日は暑くなるから。

直人：帽子を忘れて ハット した。なんちゃって！

アレックス：ハハハハハ。ウケる!

武：ハット した！クスクス

瞳：ハット した!クスクス

久：ほら皆、グズグズしてると学校に遅刻するぞ！じゃあ、お父さんは先に行くからな。行ってきます。

全員：行ってらっしゃ〜い。

語彙

支度 preparations
一階 first floor
食べ始めた（食べ始める） started to eat
帽子 hat
忘れて（忘れる） forget

QUIZ
DAY 2

1. What was Hisashi doing in the morning?

   a. Making breakfast for the family
   b. Getting ready for work
   c. Reading the newspaper
   d. Washing the dishes

2. What was Akemi doing in the morning?

   a. Making breakfast for the family
   b. Getting ready for work
   c. Reading the newspaper
   d. Washing the dishes

3. What time will Rei come home?

   a. At 5:00 sharp
   b. Around 5:00
   c. At 6:00 sharp
   d. Around 6:00

4. What is the translation of 部活(ぶかつ)?

   a. Club activities
   b. Tutoring
   c. Homeroom
   d. A-hour

5. What is the translation of "uhhh…"?

   a. うん
   b. ううん
   c. う〜ん
   d. はい

6. What is the translation of なんちゃって?

   a. C'mon
   b. What?
   c. Don't you think?
   d. Just kidding

7. Fill in the blanks to complete the sentence:
   A: この椅子はすごいね！(このいすはすごいね！)
   B: うん、ナイス椅子。___！(うん、ナイスいす。___！)

   a. えっと
   b. なんちゃって
   c. え〜
   d. うんん

8. Fill in the blanks to complete the sentence:
   A: 明日、ジムに来る？(あした、じむにくる？)
   B: ___、もちろんだよ！毎日ジムに行くから！(___、もちろんだよ！まいにちにいくから)

   a. うん
   b. ううん
   c. う〜ん
   d. え〜

9. Why does Akmi want Naoto to bring his hat?
    a. It is part of his school uniform
    b. It is going to be hot today
    c. He looks better with it
    d. To keep the sun out of his eyes

10. Who left the house first this morning?
    a. Akemi
    b. Hiromi
    c. Hisashi
    d. Takeshi

第三章
アレックス の 高校

アレックス は玲と同じ高校に通っている。二人は家の前からスクールバスで学校に行く。玲は１６歳なので高校２年生、アレックス は１５歳なので高校１年生だ。アレックス は、親友の クロエ と一緒に日本語の授業を とっている。二人は仲の良い友達だ。

１時間目の授業：日本語

アレックス：クロエ、宿題やってきた？

クロエ：もちろん！アレックス は？

アレックス：宿題やったんだけど、「は」（わ）と「が」の使い方が、いまいちまだ分かんないんだよね。

クロエ：そうそう、あと「に」と「で」の使い方、超難しくない？

アレックス：そう、オレ も マジ でわかんねー！

先生：こら!クロエとアレックス!二人でコソコソ話してないで、授業に集中しなさい!

アレックス＆クロエ：ごめんなさ～い。

語彙

高校 high school
親友 new friend
授業 class
宿題 homework
集中しなさい concentrate

QUIZ
DAY 3

1. True or False: Rei and Alex attend the same school.
   a. True
   b. False

2. True or False: Rei and Alex are in the same grade.
   a. True
   b. False

3. What period does Alex have his Japanese class?
   a. First
   b. Second
   c. Third
   d. Fourth

4. What is the translation of マジ?
   a. Extremely
   b. Well then
   c. I agree
   d. Serious

5. What is the translation of 超?

    a. Extremely
    b. Well then
    c. Serious
    d. I agree

6. Fill in the blanks to complete the sentence:

    A: その映画は___面白かったね！(そのえいがは___おもしろかったね！)
    B: うん、俺はずっと笑ってた！(うん、おれはずっとわらってた！)

    a. 当
    b. 超
    c. 著
    d. 緒

7. Fill in the blanks to complete the sentence:

    A: トムとサリーは離婚するって(トムとサリーはりこんするって)
    B: えっ、___で言ってるの？(えっ、___でいってるの？)

    a. マヅ
    b. マジ
    c. 超
    d. 本当

8. Which is the correct translation of "yesterday was super fun!"?
   a. 昨日は超楽しかった！（きのうはちょうたのしかった！）
   b. 今日は超楽しい！（きょうはちょうたのしい！）
   c. 昨日はちょっと楽しかった！（きのうはちょっとたのしかった！）
   d. 今日は超楽しかった！（ようはちょうたのしかった！）

9. True or False: Both Alex and Kuroe did their homework.
   a. True
   b. False

10. What does Alex not understand about Japanese?
   a. How to read it
   b. The difference between「は」and「が」
   c. The difference between「に」and「で」
   d. How to write it

第四章

スーパー

明美は近所の スーパー で働いている。明美の上司はあまり良い人ではないが、スーパー に来るお客さんが良い人ばかりなので、明美はお客さんとの会話を楽しむために スーパー に来ている。

明美は レジ で、近くに住むおばさん（塚本さん）と話をしていた。

塚本さん：最近ね、猫の タマ が、ぽっちゃりしてきたのよ。

明美：そうなんですか？

塚本さん：こないだね、タマ が、フェンス の外に行こうと思って、無理やり フェンス を押したのよ。バリッという音がしたと思ったら、フェンス が壊れて、タマ の首が引っかかって、取れなくなったのよ。タマ ったら、本当にかわいそうな顔をしていたわ。

語彙

近所 neighbourhood
上司 boss
会話 conversation
楽しむ to enjoy
レジ cash register

QUIZ
DAY 4

1. Where does Akemi work?

    a. She works from home
    b. At the bank
    c. At Rei's school
    d. At the supermarket

2. What does Akemi like about her job?

    a. Talking with her boss
    b. Talking with her co-workers
    c. Talking with her customers
    d. The discounts she gets

3. Where did the conversation between Akemi and the customer take place?

    a. At the door
    b. Near the cash register
    c. Outside
    d. In her office

4. What is the translation of こないだ?

    a. Serious
    b. Yesterday
    c. This space
    d. The other day

5. What is the translation of "to be chubby"?

   a. ぽっちゃりする
   b. ぴったりする
   c. ぼっちゃりする
   d. ぼちぼち

6. What is 「こないだ」short for?

   a. このあいだ
   b. こんないだ
   c. このないだ
   d. こんいだ

7. Which is the correct translation of "the other day, I went to the store"?

   a. この間、ストらに行きます（このあいだ、ストアにいきます）
   b. 昨日、ストアに行きました（きのう、ストアにいきました）
   c. この間、ストアに行きました（このあいだ、ストアにいきました）
   d. 明日、ストアに行きます（あした、ストアにいきます）

8. Fill in the blanks to complete the sentence: 私の猫は＿＿。（わたしのねこは＿＿）My cat is chubby.

   a. ぽっちゃりしない
   b. ぽっちゃりしていない
   c. ぽっちゃりしていた
   d. ぽっちゃりしている

9. What is the name of Mrs Tsukamoto's cat?

   a. Bocchi
   b. Tama
   c. Tarou
   d. Goro

10. What did Mrs Tsukamoto's cat break?

   a. The wall
   b. His collar
   c. The window
   d. The fence

第五章
久のカフェ

久はカフェを経営している。メニューには、シーフードピラフ、オムライス、ミートソースのスパゲッティ、たらこスパゲッティとカレーがある。カフェは、いつも忙しく、皆バタバタしている。

今日は、新人にメニューの注文の取り方を教えていた。

久：山田さん、おはようございます。おかえりなさい。

新人：いらっしゃいませ。

お客さん（山田さん）：久さん、おはようございます。え〜っと、じゃあ今日は、カプチーノとシーフードピラフをお願いします。

新人：はい、かしこまりました。

久：カプチーノとシーフードピラフをここに書いてね。

新人:はい、わかりました。

久:山田さん、温泉旅行はどうでしたか?

お客さん:とても良かったですよ。特に、兵庫県の城崎温泉、北海道の登別温泉、函館の湯の川温泉は最高でした!また、温泉の旅に行きたいですね!

語彙

経営している managing

カレー curry

新人 newcomer, new employee

カプチーノ cappuccino

かしこまりました certainly (used by workers towards customers)

QUIZ
DAY 5

1. What is Hisashi's job?

    a. He manages a cafe
    b. He manages a bank
    c. He manages a shop
    d. He manages an office

2. True or False: Hisashi's workplace is not busy often.

    a. True
    b. False

3. What did Mr Yamada order?

    a. A latte and a sandwich
    b. Steak and eggs
    c. A cappuccino and seafood pilaf
    d. Curry and spaghetti

4. What is the translation of バタバタする?

    a. To be tired
    b. To rush around
    c. To smile from ear to ear
    d. To struggle with something

5. What is the translation of "ummm…" in Japanese?

    a. それ
    b. えっと
    c. なっとう
    d. じつは

6. Fill in the blanks to complete the sentence:
    A: パーティーに何人くらい来た？(パーティーになんにんくらいきた？)
    B: ___。。。10人くらいかな。(___。。。１０にんくらいかな)

    a. それ
    b. えっと
    c. なっとう
    d. バタバタした

7. What is the Japanese translation of "I was busy all day today!"?

    a. 今日、ずっとバタバタしている！(きょう、ずっとバタバタしている！)
    b. 昨日、ずっとバタバタしている！(きのう、ずっとタバタしている！)
    c. 昨日、ずっとバタバタしていた！(きのう、ずっとばたばたしていた！)
    d. 今日、ずっとバタバタしていた！(きょう、ずっとばたばたしていた！)

8. True or False:「えっと」is formal Japanese.

    a. True
    b. False

9. What was Hisashi doing?

    a. Training a new employee
    b. Cooking food
    c. Making drinks
    d. Filing papers

10. Where did Mr Yamada come back from?

    a. A vacation
    b. His office
    c. The park
    d. His hometown

第六章
祖父母の銭湯

子供達のおじいちゃんとおばあちゃんは、近所で銭湯を経営している。銭湯のお客さんは毎年減り、祖父母は困っていた。

アレックス は、おじいちゃんとおばあちゃんの銭湯に来た。6ヶ月前に日本に来たアレックス は、まだ銭湯に来たことがなかった。銭湯の古いドア が ガラッと開いた。

アレックス：こんばんは。

祖母：あら、アレックス さん、こんばんは。

祖父：アレックス さん、来てくれてありがとう。好きなだけ入っておいで。

アレックス：ありがとうございます。

お客さん：どこの国の人だい？

アレックス：イギリス人です。今、小林家で ホームステイ を しています。今日が銭湯初めてなんです。

お客さん：そうかい、じゃあ、ここで服を全部脱いだら、ついてきなさい。

アレックス：え〜??あっ、はい

語彙

銭湯 bathhouse
毎年 every year
困っていた was worried
古い old
服 clothing

QUIZ
DAY 6

1. What is happening to the number of customers at the public bath?

    a. It is the same as always
    b. It is increasing every year
    c. It is decreasing every year
    d. No more customers come at all

2. When did Alex come to Japan?

    a. 2 months ago
    b. 6 months ago
    c. 1 year ago
    d. 2 years ago

3. True or False: Alex has been to many public baths in Japan.

    a. True
    b. False

4. What is the word to describe something opening suddenly?

    a. ガラ
    b. カラ
    c. コラ
    d. ゴラ

5. What is an 音喩?

    a. A short sentence
    b. A word used to describe a movement
    c. An expression of surprise
    d. A palindrome

6. Which word can we translate as "ummm…"?

    a. え〜
    b. うん
    c. ううん
    d. えっと

7. Fill in the blanks to complete the sentence: スーパーのドアが___と開いた (スーパーのドアが___とひらいた)

    a. とても
    b. ガラ
    c. え〜
    d. 超

8. Fill in the blanks to complete the sentence:

    A: その人知ってる？(そのひとしってる？) Do you know him?
    B: ___、知らないよ。(___、しらないよ) No, I don't.
    a. うん
    b. え〜
    c. ううん
    d. えっと

9. Where is Alex from?

   a. Canada
   b. Japan
   c. England
   d. America

10. Why is Alex surprised at the end?

    a. The bath is more expensive than he thought
    b. The bath is used by both men and women
    c. The old man knows his father
    d. He has to take off all of his clothes

第七章
お盆休み

夕方、久は明美にお盆休みの旅行を提案した。久はこの温泉旅行が、両親の ビジネス を助ける ヒント になるのではないかと考えていた。明美はもちろん!と答えた。小林家の家族皆が夕食を食べ始めた。明美は嬉しそうに ニコニコ している。

玲：お母さんどうしたのそんなに ニコニコ して。

明美：お盆休みね、皆で家族旅行に行くことにしたの。

直人：え〜マジ で〜、やった〜!

アレックス：どこに行くんですか?

久：兵庫県と北海道だ。 アレックス君も一緒に来るといい。君の分も出してあげるから。

アレックス：本当にいいんですか!?ありがとうございます!

直人：旅行気分は良好！

武 & 瞳 & クロ：ムシャ、ムシャ

語彙

夕方 evening
提案した proposed
両親 parents
気分 feeling
良好 good, excellent

QUIZ
DAY 7

1. What were Hisashi and Akemi doing together?

    a. Having breakfast
    b. Having lunch
    c. Discussing their days
    d. Planning a trip

2. Why did Hisashi think going on a trip would be a good thing?

    a. He could finally relax
    b. He might learn something to help his parents' business
    c. Alex will get to experience more of Japan
    d. It will help get his family out of the house

3. Why was Akemi smiling?

    a. Her food was really good
    b. Takeshi told a funny joke
    c. She thought of something funny that happened that day
    d. She is happy to be planning a trip

4. Fill in the blanks to complete the sentence: 友達のトム___は優しい（ともだちの___はやさしい）My friend Tom is nice.

   a. 君
   b. 岩
   c. 海
   d. 屋

5. Fill in the blanks to complete the sentence: ___はどこに行くの？（___は'どこにいくの？）Where are you going?

   a. 君
   b. 彼
   c. 彼女
   d. 私

6. True or False: 君 can only be used with boys.

   a. True
   b. False

7. What is the translation of ニコニコ

   a. With a wink
   b. With a grin
   c. With a frown
   d. With a tear

8. Which is the correct translation of あの猫はニコニコしていた (あのねこはニコニコしていた)?

    a. This cat was smiling
    b. That cat is smiling
    c. That cat smiles
    d. That cat was smiling

9. Where are they going for their trip?

    a. Hyouga Prefecture and Hokkaido
    b. Tokyo and Kyoto
    c. Nagasaki and Fukuoka
    d. Tokyo and Hokkaido

10. True or False: Alex needs to use his own money for the trip.

    a. True
    b. False

第八章
旅行の準備

明美の家族は、お盆休みの温泉旅行に行く支度をしていた。明美は武と瞳の服をスーツケースに入れ、子供達は自分のスーツケースに荷物を入れた。初めての旅行なので、子供達は何を持っていくべきか考えながら荷物を詰めた。

直人：ワクワクする！これも持って行こうっと。

玲：ヤバイ直人、そんなのいらないって！

直人：お姉ちゃんだって、こんなのいらないじゃん！

玲：直人、ウザイ！あ〜、おしっこ、ちょっとトイレ行ってくる。

直人：早くトイレに行っといれ

玲：また、始まった！

語彙

準備 preparations

にもつ荷物 luggage

い入れた put inside

かんが考えながら while thinking

トイレ bathroom, toilet

QUIZ
DAY 8

1. What did Akemi do for the twins?

    a. She packed their lunches
    b. She packed their clothes
    c. She helped them get dressed
    d. She made them breakfast

2. The children have been on a trip before.

    a. True
    b. False

3. How does Naoto feel about going on a trip?

    a. He is nervous
    b. He is upset
    c. He is indifferent
    d. He is excited

4. What is the translation of ヤバイ?

    a. Sweet
    b. Dangerous
    c. Funny
    d. Loud

5. Fill in the blanks to complete the sentence: 好きじゃない？このセーターはかわいい___。(すきじゃない？このセーターはかわいい___)

   a. 君
   b. じゃん
   c. あなた
   d. そう

6. What is the translation of ワクワクする?

   a. To be hungry
   b. To be upset
   c. To be tired
   d. To be excited

7. Translate the following into Japanese: The boy is excited.

   a. あの男の子がワクワクしている (あのおとこのこがワクワクしている)
   b. 男の子たちがワクワクしている (おとこのこたちがワクワクしている)
   c. あの男の子がワクワクしていた (あのおとこのこがワクワクしていた)
   d. 男の子たちがワクワクした (おとこのこたちがワクワクした)

8. Translate the following sentence into Japanese: "Oh no! There's no time!"

   a. ヤバイ！時間がない！(ヤバイ！じかんがない！)
   b. やっぱり！時間がない！(やっぱり！じかんがない！)
   c. ヤバイ！時間がなかった！(ヤバイ！じかんがなかった！)
   d. やっぱり！時間がなかった！(やっぱり！じかんがなかった！)

9. What were Naoto and Rei fighting over?

   a. What kinds of clothes they should wear
   b. Who would sit next to the window
   c. What to pack
   d. How long the trip would take

10. Where does Rei go?

    a. She goes to her room to get her clothes
    b. She goes to the kitchen
    c. She goes to the bathroom
    d. She goes outside

第九章
出発

朝になり、小林家一行は、東京駅へ向かった。新幹線で東京駅から京都駅へと行くためだ。

子供達は新幹線が初めてなので、ドキドキしていた。席についてしばらくすると、窓から奇麗な景色が見えてきた。

玲：あ、富士山だ!

武＆瞳：わあ〜!

明美：富士山は日本で一番高い山よ。

直人：あれは何?

久：あれは、静岡の茶畑だ。ほら、おばさん達がお茶の葉を摘んでいるだろ?緑色の茶畑と、青い空のコントラストが奇麗だな。

アレックス：本当ですね!

語彙(ごい)

出発(しゅっぱつ) taking off, depart
駅(えき) station
新幹線(しんかんせん) bullet train
席(せき) seat
窓(まど) window

QUIZ
DAY 9

1. Where was the family headed in the morning?

    a. Hyouga station
    b. Nagasaki station
    c. Hokkaido station
    d. Tokyo station

2. How was the family travelling?

    a. By plane
    b. By car
    c. By bus
    d. By bullet train

3. What could be seen from the windows?

    a. Mt. Fuji
    b. The stars
    c. Tall skyscrapers
    d. A waterfall

4. True or False:「だ」is more formal than「です」

    a. True
    b. False

5. What is the translation of ドキドキする?

    a. To be sleepy
    b. To be tired
    c. To be anxious
    d. To be angry

6. Fill in the blanks to complete the sentence: 全然勉強してない。もうすぐ試験が始まるけど。。。___している（ぜんぜんべんきょうしてない。もうすぐしけんがはじまるけど。。。___している）

    a. クスクス
    b. ワクワク
    c. ドキドキ
    d. ゴロゴロ

7. Translate the following sentence into Japanese: I was anxious.

    a. ドキドキしている
    b. ドキドキしていた
    c. ドキドキする
    d. ワクワクする

8. Fill in the blanks to complete the sentence: 明日東京に行きます！___するね！（あしたとうきょうにいきます！___するね！）

    a. クスクス
    b. ワクワク
    c. バラバラ
    d. ゴロゴロ

9. Mt. Fuji is the tallest mountain in Japan.

    a. True
    b. False

10. According to Hisashi, what makes a beautiful contrast with the green tea fields?

    a. Mt. Fuji
    b. The clear water
    c. The blue sky
    d. The old ladies in the field

第十章
京都

小林家一行は、京都駅に着いた。京都着の新幹線は少し早く着いた。荷物が沢山あったので、京都駅から タクシー で旅館まで行った。部屋で少し休んでから、旅館の中にある食堂で昼ご飯を食べることにした。

直人：あ〜お腹空いた〜!

ウエイトレス：おいでやす。ご注文はお決まりですか?

明美：はい、お子様ランチ二つと、豆腐定食二つ。それと、にしんそば二つお願いします。アレックス さんは?

アレックス：ぼくも豆腐定食にします。

ウエイトレス：はい、かしこまりました。

アレックス：京都は豆腐が有名だから、ホカホカ の湯豆腐が楽しみです!

語彙(ごい)

着(つ)いた arrived
沢山(たくさん) many
部屋(へや) room
食堂(しょくどう) cafeteria, dining area
ご注文(ちゅうもん) order

QUIZ
DAY 10

1. What city is the family in now?

    a. Kyoto
    b. Tokyo
    c. Nagano
    d. Okinawa

2. How did the family get from the station to the *ryokan*?

    a. By bus
    b. By train
    c. They walked
    d. By taxi

3. Where did the family eat lunch?

    a. In their room
    b. At a restaurant inside their *ryokan*
    c. At a restaurant outside of their *ryokan*
    d. They did not have time to eat lunch

4. What will employees of a business in Kyoto likely say to welcome you to their business?

    a. おやすみ
    b. んちゃ〜
    c. おいでやす
    d. お疲れ様です

5. What is the translation of ホカホカ?

   a. Smilingly
   b. Floating
   c. Steaming hot
   d. Being nervous

6. True or False:「おいでやす」is an expression commonly used all throughout Japan.

   a. True
   b. False

7. Translate the following in Japanese: "Steaming hot curry".

   a. 辛いカレー（からいカレー）
   b. 苦いカレー（にがいカレー）
   c. ホカホカするカレー
   d. 冷たいカレー（つめたいカレー）

8. In Tokyo, instead of「おいでやす」what expression might an employee at a restaurant use to greet you?

   a. お疲れ様です（おつかれさまです）
   b. すみません
   c. なるほど
   d. いらっしゃいませ

9. How many orders of nishin soba did the family order?

   a. 1
   b. 2
   c. 3
   d. 4

10. What does Alex order?
    a. Soba
    b. A lunch set
    c. Ramen
    d. Boiled tofu

第十一章
芸者さん

昼ご飯を食べた後、小林家一行は、祇園へ芸者さんに会いに行った。芸者さんは、奇麗な着物を着て、シャランシャランと髪飾りの音を鳴らしながら、祇園の街を歩いていた。コツンコツンという下駄の音も聞こえた。

久：すみません。一緒に写真撮ってもいいですか？

明美：お父さんやだ〜、はずい！

芸者さん：いいどすえ。

明美：え、いいんですか？ありがとうございます！おおきに。

玲：お母さん、イントネーション違うっしょ。

明美：すみません、写真撮ってもらえますか？

道を歩いていた人：はい、いいですよ。はい チーズ。

[カチャ]

小林家（こばやしけ）：ありがとうございました！

芸者（げいしゃ）さん：ほな、ごきげんよう。

語彙（ごい）

会（あ）いに行（い）った went to meet
綺麗（きれい） pretty, nice looking
音（おと） sound
歩（ある）いてた was walking

イントネーション intonation

QUIZ
DAY 11

1. After eating lunch, where did the Kobayashi family go?

   a. To Gion
   b. To the mall
   c. To a hot spring
   d. To karaoke

2. How did Akemi feel when Hisashi asked the geisha to take a photo?

   a. She was happy
   b. She was angry
   c. She was embarrassed
   d. She was indifferent

3. After being asked to take a photo, the geisha says no to Hisashi.

   a. True
   b. False

4. What is a more informal way of saying「恥ずかしい」(はずかしい)?

   a. キモイ
   b. ビミョウ
   c. ワニ
   d. ハズイ

5. What is the translation of 「どすえ」?

   a. Wouldn't you agree?
   b. Or whatever
   c. I assure you it is so
   d. Probably

6. In Kansai, instead of 「ありがとうございます」, what might one say?

   a. ほんまやな
   b. おおきに
   c. でやす
   d. どすえ

7. Fill in the blanks to complete the sentence:
   A:　お父さん!そんなことを私の友達に言わないで!＿＿＿よ!（おとうさん!そんなことをわたしのともだちにいわないで!）＿＿＿よ!)

   a. メラメラ
   b. ゴロゴロ
   c. バイバイ
   d. ハズイ

8. Fill in the blanks to complete the sentence:
   A: 私の一番好きな寺は金閣寺＿＿＿。（わたしのいちばんすきなてらはきんかくじ＿＿＿。）

   a. なら
   b. とはいえ
   c. どすえ
   d. それゆえに

9. Rei thinks that her mother speaks the Kyoto dialect very well.

   a. True
   b. False

10. Who took the photo?

    a. Akemi
    b. Hisashi
    c. The geisha
    d. A stranger

第十二章
お寺

小林家族は、祇園で芸者さんと一緒に写真を取ってもらった後、金閣寺、銀閣寺、清水寺に行った。清水寺には三つの滝があった。

久：これは三条の滝といって、これが学問、真ん中が恋、あっちが健康のご利益があるんだ。一つだけにしないと、ご利益を授かることはできないんだよ。

玲：え～！じゃあ私は真ん中の恋愛！

アレックス：え～っと、じゃあ僕は、学問にしよっと。

明美：じゃあ、私は健康。

久：俺も真ん中の恋だな。

[パ～ンチ]

久：いてぇ!明美、冗談だよ。俺は、お前しか愛していないからな。

直人：おえ〜!

玲：マジ、キモイ。

語彙

写真 photo
滝 waterfall
健康 health
利益 profits
冗談 joke

QUIZ
DAY 12

1. After getting their photo with the geisha, where did the Kobayashi family go?

    a. They went to see temples
    b. They went to a hot spring
    c. They went shopping
    d. They went to a museum

2. How many waterfalls can be found at Kiyomizu temple?

    a. 1
    b. 2
    c. 3
    d. 4

3. Which waterfall does Rei choose?

    a. The waterfall of study and learning
    b. The waterfall of love
    c. The waterfall of health
    d. She does not choose a waterfall

4. What is the translation of the word 「お前」?

    a. You
    b. We
    c. He
    d. She

5. The word「お前」is considered formal Japanese.

   a. True
   b. False

6. Which is a shortened form of the expression 「気持ち悪い」(きもちわるい)?

   a. カブト
   b. キチイ
   c. キモイ
   d. カメハメハ

7. Fill in the blanks to complete the sentence: ___は誰だ？(___はだれだ？) (Who are you?).

   a. 彼（かれ）
   b. お前（おまえ）
   c. 俺（ぼく）
   d. 僕（おれ）

8. Fill in the blank to complete the sentence: ああ〜ゴキブリがいる！___！ (Hint: ゴキブリ = "cockroach").

   a. キモイ
   b. お前
   c. どすえ
   d. バタバタ

9. Which waterfall does Alex choose?

    a. The waterfall of study and learning
    b. The waterfall of love
    c. The waterfall of health
    d. He does not choose a waterfall

10. In the end, Hisashi chose the waterfall of love.

    a. True
    b. False

第十三章
五山送り火

小林家一行は、お盆の伝統行事である五山送り火を見に行くため、東山へ向かった。夜になり、大の文字の火が見え始めた。五山送り火は、大文字の送り火や大文字焼きとも言われている。

直人：あ、いい感じで、大の漢字が見えてきた!

玲：結構いいじゃん。

久：ほんまやな

明美：お父さん、関西弁上手!

久：そんなこと、あらへんで。

玲：あ、調子に乗った。

久：大の字の送り火は、お盆の間、戻ってきたご先祖様の霊を あの世に送るためのものなんだよ。

アレックス：へえ、そうなんですね。

直人：玲の霊を送る。

玲：直人、それ微妙・・・

武：パパ、だっこ。

瞳：ひとみも。

久：しゃあないなあ。

明美：じゃあ、瞳はママが抱っこしてあげる。よいしょ。

これで、見える？

瞳：うん、見える！

語彙

伝統 traditional
感じ feeling
結構 quite, extremely
上手 skilled
調子に乗った got carried away

QUIZ
DAY 13

1. Where did the Kobayashi family go in order to see the Gozan Okuribi?

    a. Gion
    b. Higashi Yama
    c. Osaka
    d. Kinkaku Temple

2. At what time of day do the Kobayashi's watch the 大の文字の火（だいのもじのひ）?

    a. Morning
    b. Afternoon
    c. Evening
    d. They do not watch it

3. Akemi is impressed by Hisashi's Kansai dialect.

    a. True
    b. False

4. What is the translation of 感じ（かんじ）?

    a. Chinese characters
    b. A feeling
    c. A special place
    d. Time

5. In Kansai, instead of 本当（ほんとう）, what might one say?

   a. おおきに
   b. ほんま
   c. まいど
   d. どすえ

6. Upon hearing something impressive, what can one say?

   a. ううん
   b. うん
   c. えっと
   d. へえ

7. Fill in the blanks to complete the sentence: A: ねぇねえ、この___書ける？（ねぇねえ、この___かける？）

   a. 感じ（かんじ）
   b. 幹事（かんじ）
   c. 漢字（かんじ）
   d. 莞爾（かんじ）

8. Fill in the blanks to complete the sentence:
   A: トムさんは四年間くらい日本に住んだ（とむさんはよんねんかんくらいにほんにすんだ）
   B: ___すごい。だから彼の日本語はあんなに上手だね（___すごい。だらｋかれのにほんごはあんなにじょうずだね）

   a. おい
   b. えっと
   c. へえ
   d. そう

9. Who does Hisashi hold in his arms?

   a. Hitomi
   b. Akemi
   c. Alex
   d. Takeshi

10. Who does Akemi hold in her arms?

    a. Hitomi
    b. Akemi
    c. Alex
    d. Takeshi

第十四章
京都最終日

次の日の朝、小林家一行は、京都の旅館に荷物を置いて、嵐山に行った。嵐山で保津川下りを楽しむためだ。

小林家：キャー！

川下りのベテラン：皆さん、船にしっかり捕まってください。

直人：ワイは怖い！

小林家：キャー！

————————————————————

川下りの後、嵐山の食堂に入り、京都で有名な湯葉、おでん、抹茶アイスを注文した。

久：おでんのダシがきいてるやん。

玲：お父さん、はずいから関西弁使おうとするのやめて！

明美：湯葉も美味しい！あなた達はいつつも、ポテチ とか チョコ ばっかり食べてるから、こういう時に、体に良い大豆料理を沢山食べておきなさい。

語彙

船 ship, boat
捕まって hold onto
怖い scary
有名 famous, well-known
抹茶 green tea

QUIZ
DAY 14

1. Where did the Kobayashi family leave their luggage?

    a. They forgot it on the bus
    b. At the ryokan
    c. At the station
    d. They brought their luggage with them

2. How did the family get to Mount Arashi?

    a. By boat
    b. By foot
    c. By plane
    d. By train

3. How did Naoto feel on the way to Mount Arashi?

    a. Nervous
    b. Happy
    c. Sad
    d. Scared

4. What is the translation of ワイ?

    a. You
    b. I
    c. He
    d. We

5. What is the shortened form of ポテトチップス?

   a. ポテト
   b. ポト
   c. トッチ
   d. ポテチ

6. What is the shortened form of チョコレート?

   a. チョッコ
   b. チョコ
   c. コレー
   d. レート

7. What is the shortened form of McDonald's?

   a. マック
   b. マク
   c. ムク
   d. ムック

8. What is the shortened form of Starbucks?

   a. スターバ
   b. スタバー
   c. スタバ
   d. スッタバ

9. What kind of ice cream is famous in Kyoto?

   a. Green Tea
   b. Chocolate
   c. Tofu
   d. Sweet Bean

10. Why does Akemi want everyone to eat soy-based food?
    a. It tastes better than chocolate
    b. It is healthy
    c. They do not have the opportunity often
    d. It tastes better than potato chips

第十五章
兵庫県

次の日の朝、小林家一行は、兵庫県の城崎温泉に行くため、旅館を出て京都駅へ向かった。日本三景の一つである天橋立が途中にあるので、京都駅から高速バスに乗って、まずは天橋立に行った。

玲：わあ〜、キレイ!

直人：天国に上る橋みたい!玲の霊を送る。

玲：直人、ガチウザイ。ちょっとキレていい?

[ゴツン]

直人：いってー!姉ちゃんに殴られた〜。

久：二人ともやめなさい!天橋立は、3千年前にできたと言われているんだよ。

アレックス：へえ〜、歴史が古いんですね。

明美：周りには、5千本から8千本の松の木が生えているんですって。

語彙

県 prefecture
向かった headed toward
天国 heaven
霊 soul, ghost
殴られた was hit

QUIZ
DAY 15

1. After leaving the ryokan, where did the Kobayashi family head?

   a. To the onsen
   b. To Kyoto station
   c. To the mall
   d. To a nearby park

2. Where did the Kobayashi family take the express bus to?

   a. 天国（てんごく）
   b. 京都駅（きょうとえき）
   c. 天橋立（あまのはしだて）
   d. 公園（こうえん）

3. True or False: The bridge goes to heaven.

   a. True
   b. False

4. What is the translation of「ガチウザイ」?

   a. Slightly disheartening
   b. Extremely funny
   c. Extremely annoying
   d. Slightly sad

5. True or False: 「ガチ」is similar in meaning to 「本当に」 and 「本気で」?

   a. True
   b. False

6. What is the translation of 「キレる」?

   a. To hit
   b. To cut
   c. To get angry
   d. To be scared

7. Which of the following represents the sound of being hit?

   a. フラフラ
   b. ゴツン
   c. シン
   d. メラメラ

8. According to the lesson, [いってー] is a more colloquial word for which of the following?

   a. いって
   b. いてた
   c. いたい
   d. いった

9. True or False: Rei thought Naoto's joke was funny.

   a. True
   b. False

10. According to legend, how long ago was 天橋立 (あまのはしだて) constructed?

    a. 1000 years
    b. 2000 years
    c. 3000 years
    d. 4000 years

第十六章
城崎温泉

小林一家は、天橋立から電車で城崎温泉に着いた。一行は、旅館に荷物を置いてから、早速、温泉へと向かった。一日入り放題の温泉券を買ったので、城崎温泉内にある温泉に入れるだけ入ることができる。レストランの食べ放題と同じだ。皆、城崎温泉内にある七つの温泉に全て入ろうと意気込んでいた。

明美、玲、瞳は一の湯の女湯に、アレックス、久、直人、武は男湯に入った。

直人：僕が一番!

久：直人、待ちなさい。

アレックス：僕が先に入りますから、久さんは武君といてください。

久：ありがとう。

アレックス：直人君、湯舟に入る前に、体を洗わなきゃ駄目だよ。ゴシゴシ洗わなくてもいいから、お湯を ザッとかけるだけでいい。

直人：そんなこと、知ってるもん！

アレックス：おじいちゃんとおばあちゃんの銭湯に行った時、お客さんに教えてもらったんだ。

語彙

電車 train
早速 at once, immediately
食べ放題 all-you-can-eat
女湯 bath for ladies
男湯 bath for men

QUIZ
DAY 16

1. Where did the family go after dropping their luggage off at the hotel?

    a. They went to a restaurant
    b. They went shopping
    c. They went to their rooms to take a nap
    d. They went to an onsen

2. True or False: Today, the Kobayashi family can go in and out of the Kinosaki Onsens as much as they want.

    a. True
    b. False

3. At what kind of restaurant did the Kobayashi family eat?

    a. Japanese restaurant
    b. A salad bar
    c. An all-you-can-eat restaurant
    d. A fast-food restaurant

4. This is often added to the ends of sentences to sound cute.

    a. です
    b. でした
    c. でございます
    d. もん

5. What is the translation of ゴシゴシ?

   a. Dirty
   b. Scrub hard
   c. Move slowly
   d. Roll around

6. Fill in the blanks to complete the sentence:
   A: やっぱり、お前かわいいのが好きね(やっぱり、お前かわいいのがすきね)
   B: だって、女の子だ___(だって、おんなのこだ___)

   a. あります
   b. でした
   c. です
   d. もん

7. Fill in the blanks to complete the sentence: 顔は汚れているから、___洗わないといけない(かおはよごれているから、___あわないといけない)

   a. ポツポツ
   b. ゴシゴシ
   c. メラメラ
   d. ギラギラ

8. Fill in the blanks to complete the sentence: それを___と見てすぐ分かった(それを___とみてすぐわかった)

   a. サ
   b. ザ
   c. サッ
   d. ザッ

9. How many onsens, in total, are there within Kinosaki Onsen?

   a. 4
   b. 5
   c. 6
   d. 7

10. According to Alex, what must one do before going into the bathtub?

    a. Pay the entry fee
    b. Wash one's body
    c. Secure one's belongings in the lockers
    d. Put on one's slippers

第十七章
城崎温泉の夜

小林一家は、一日中温泉を楽しんだ後、旅館の食堂で夕食を食べていた。

明美：バタバタ忙しかったけど、全部入れたね。

久：城崎温泉では、7つの温泉全てに入ることができると、夫婦円満、不老不死、試験合格、商売繁盛が叶うと言われているんだよ。

明美：おじいちゃんとおばあちゃんの商売繁盛が叶うといいわ。

久：そうだな。銭湯より、やっぱり温泉の方が商売になると思う。

直人：ほんまやな。

玲：ガキ、うるさい。

直人：うるさい サイ

[ボコッ]

直人：いった～い！姉ちゃんに殴られた！

明美：二人ともいい加減にしなさい！

語彙

一日中 all day
叶う to come true (of a wish or prayer)
言われている it is said
うるさい noisy, shut up
いい加減にしなさい act properly

QUIZ
DAY 17

1. What did the Kobayashi family do after visiting the hot springs?

    a. They went to bed
    b. They flew back home
    c. They ate dinner
    d. They went to the theatre

2. True or False: The Kobayashi's were able to visit all of the onsens.

    a. True
    b. False

3. In total, how many onsens were there to visit?

    a. 5
    b. 6
    c. 7
    d. 8

4. Translate the following sentence into English: 今日、私は一日中バタバタしていた。(今日、わたしはいちにちじゅうバタバタしていた)

    a. I was busy all day yesterday
    b. He was busy all day
    c. I was busy all day today
    d. I was busy this morning

5. When you want to tell someone to shut up, what can you say?

   a. うるさい
   b. いいよ
   c. 聞こえない (きこえない)
   d. なるほど

6. Which word has the same meaning as the Kansai word 「ほんま」?

   a. 本戸 (ほんと)
   b. 本部 (ほんぶ)
   c. 本棚 (ほんだな)
   d. 本当 (ほんとう)

7. Fill in the blanks to complete the sentence: このカフェはちょっと＿＿ね。ちゃんと会話できない。(このかふぇはちょっと＿＿ね。ちゃんと会話できない)

   a. 楽しい (たのしい)
   b. 高い (たかい)
   c. 安い (やすい)
   d. うるさい

8. Fill in the blanks to complete the sentence: 今日ずっと＿＿ていたから疲れているよ。(きょうずっと＿＿していたからつかれているよ)

   a. ヘラヘラ
   b. バタバタ
   c. パラパラ
   d. クスクス

9. True or False: Hisashi thinks that opening an onsen would be a good business decision.

    a. True
    b. False

10. Who hit Naoto?

    a. Akemi
    b. Alex
    c. Hisashi
    d. Rei

第十八章
初めての飛行機

次の日の朝、小林一家は城崎温泉を出て、大阪の空港へと向かった。子供達は飛行機に乗るのが初めてだったので興奮していた。

明美：お父さん、武と瞳のシートベルトしてあげて。

[カチッ]

武：やだー、ぼくしない。

久：飛行機に乗る時は、シートベルトをしなきゃならないんだよ。少し緩めてあげるから。ほら、大丈夫だろ？

アレックス：直人君、窓から富士山が見えるかもしれないよ。

直人：えーマジでー！

隣の人：ほな、おじさん席変わってあげる。

アレックス：いいんですか？ありがとうございます。直人君もおじさんにお礼を言って。

直人：おおきに、気に入った！

語彙

飛行機 aeroplane
空港 airport
興奮していた was excited
シートベルト seat belt
礼 thanks, gratitude

QUIZ
DAY 18

1. Where did the Kobayashi family go in the morning?

    a. The airport
    b. The bus station
    c. The train station
    d. To a nearby cafe

2. True or False: This was the first time that the children have ridden in an aeroplane.

    a. True
    b. False

3. What did Hisashi do for the kids?

    a. He carried their bags
    b. He helped buckle their seatbelts
    c. He put their bags in the overhead bin
    d. He put on a movie

4. Which word can translate to "it is true" or "really"?

    a. まじで
    b. ほな
    c. おおきに
    d. ほか

5. True or False: 「ほな」 is standard Japanese used throughout the country.

   a. True
   b. False

6. How would one say 「ありがとう」 using Kansai dialect?

   a. まじで
   b. ほな
   c. おおきに
   d. ほら

7. Fill in the blanks to complete the sentence:
   A: このラーメンは美味しくない (このラーメンはおいしくない)
   B: ___、オレのを食べてみて (___、おれのをたべみて)

   a. まじで
   b. ほな
   c. おおきに
   d. ほか

8. Fill in the blanks to complete the sentence:
   A: やばい!
   B: どうしたの?
   A: お母さんが___怒ってるよ。(おかあさんが___おこってるよ)

   a. まじで
   b. ほな
   c. おおきに
   d. ほか

9. What could be seen from the window?
    a. Birds
    b. The city skyline
    c. The ocean
    d. Mt. Fuji

10. What did the old man do?
    a. He helped take a picture
    b. He took a nap
    c. He switched seats with Naoto
    d. He told Naoto an interesting story

第十九章
札幌

小林一家は、札幌に着いた後、空港でレンタカーを借りて、函館に向かった。途中、道の駅で、イモ団子やソフトクリームを食べて休憩した。

皆お腹が空いたので、道の駅の食堂で、昼ご飯を食べることにした。

明美：カラッと晴れて良かったわね。東京と違ってムシムシ暑くないし。ダラダラ汗をかかなくていいし。

久：北海道はやっぱり景色が違うなあ。

お店の人：お待たせしました。塩ラーメンとイカラーメンです。

玲：わあ〜、イカが丸ごとラーメンの中に入ってる。

アレックス：イカはいかが？

直人：アレックス ずる〜い、僕の ギャグ取らないで！

久：直人、お前一本取られたな。

語彙

レンタカー rental car
休憩した took a break
景色 scenery
違う different
お待たせしました sorry for keeping you waiting

QUIZ
DAY 19

1. Where did the Kobayashi family arrive?

    a. Tokyo
    b. Osaka
    c. Nagano
    d. Sapporo

2. How did the Kobayashi's get to Hakodate?

    a. By car
    b. By bus
    c. By train
    d. By plane

3. What did the Kobayashi's do during their break on their way to Hakodate?

    a. They took a nap
    b. They had a picnic
    c. They went hiking in the mountains
    d. They had soft serve ice cream.

4. How can we describe weather that is hot and humid?

    a. マツマツ
    b. マシマシ
    c. ムツムツ
    d. ムシムシ

5. How can we describe something that is dripping or flowing heavily?

   a. ドロドロ
   b. ダラダラ
   c. ゴロゴロ
   d. ペラペラ

6. Fill in the blanks to complete the sentence: 日本は島国だから夏はやっぱり＿＿暑い (にほんはくにぐにだからなつはやっぱり＿＿あつい)

   a. だし
   b. もね
   c. むし
   d. なの

7. Fill in the blanks to complete the sentence: 彼はリンゴの皮を剥かずに＿＿食べた (かれあはりんごのかわをむかずに＿＿たべた)

   a. かなり
   b. なるほど
   c. たまに
   d. まるごと

8. Fill in the blanks to complete the sentence: お客様、こちらのジャケットは＿＿でしょうか？(おきゃくさま、こりたのじゃけっとは＿＿でしょうか？)

   a. ダラダラ
   b. いかが
   c. むし
   d. まるごと

9. What did the family eat for lunch?
    a. Sushi
    b. Okonomiyaki
    c. Ramen
    d. Sukiyaki

10. True or False: Alex took one of Nato's books.
    a. True
    b. False

第二十章
湯の川温泉

小林一家は、函館に着いた。湯の川温泉の旅館に着いた時、すでに夕食の時間になっていた。すでに温泉に入ったアレックスだけ浴衣を着ていた。

明美：わあ〜、あわびが大きい!

直人：でかでかー!

玲：いか、超美味しいー! 超新鮮!っていうか、アレックスだけ浴衣?

アレックス：もう温泉に入りました。

玲：え?

アレックス：１０分で充分です。

直人：また アレックス、ギャグ言ったー。

アレックス：今のはギャグじゃなかったんだけど・・・

明美：私なら、もっとゆっくり入るけどな。

久：せっかく温泉に来たのに、１０分はないだろう。もったいないなあ・・・

語彙

すでに already
超 extremely
充分 enough
ギャグ joke, gag
もったいない a waste of (time, money, an opportunity)

QUIZ
DAY 20

1. Where did the Kobayashi family arrive?

    a. Tokyo
    b. Hakodate
    c. Nagano
    d. Kyoto

2. What time was it when the Kobayashi's arrived at the onsen?

    a. Morning
    b. Afternoon
    c. Evening
    d. Midnight

3. What was Alex wearing?

    a. A yukata
    b. A jinbei
    c. A kimono
    d. A shirt and shorts

4. What is a translation of 超 (ちょう)?

    a. Confusing
    b. Silly
    c. Extreme
    d. Bad

5. How is the following written in Hiragana: 十分は十分です

    a. じゅぷんはじゅぶんです
    b. じゅっぷんはじゅうぶんです
    c. じゅぷんはじゅうぶんです
    d. じゅっぷんはじゅっぶんです

6. What is the translation of もったいない?

    a. It is not there
    b. Can't be held
    c. It's a waste
    d. I agree with you

7. Fill in the blanks to complete the sentence:
    A:　来週、歌舞伎を見に行くよ！(らいしゅう、かぶきをみにいくよ!)
    B: へ〜私も見たい＿＿＿ (へ〜わたしもみたい＿＿＿)

    a. ほな
    b. どすえ
    c. なあ
    d. もったいない

8. Fill in the blanks to complete the sentence:
    A:　中国に住んでたけど万里の長城に行ったことはない。(ちゅうごくにすんでたけどばんりのちょうじょうにいったことはない)
    B:　へ〜＿＿＿ね。中国に住んでたのに。(へ〜＿＿＿ね。ちゅうごくにすんでたのに)

    a. まってない
    b. もったいない
    c. もんだいない
    d. もらってない

9. What did they have for dinner?
    a. Eel
    b. Crab
    c. Abalone
    d. Shrimp

10. True or False: Hisashi thinks 10 minutes is a good amount of time to spend in an onsen.
    a. True
    b. False

第二十一章
函館観光

次の日の朝、小林家は朝一で、いかそうめん、イクラ丼を食べてから、元町に向かった。元町には坂道が沢山ある。

有名な八幡坂を上りながら、皆カシャカシャと写真を撮っている。

久：しかし絵になる景色だよなあ。

明美：本当。坂の上からの景色は最高ね!

[カシャ、カシャ]

武：ママ、おんぶ。

瞳：パパ、おんぶ。

直人：オレも、ママおんぶ。

玲：うわー、だっさー!「ママ、おんぶ」だってー。その年で。

直人：姉ちゃん、うっさい！

[パンチ]

玲：直人、痛い！

直人：さっきの仕返し。あっかんべーだ！●

久：二人ともやめなさい！

語彙

観光 tourism, sightseeing
食べてから after eating
坂道 hill road
取っている taking (photos)
絵 picture, painting

QUIZ
DAY 21

1. Before going to Motomachi, what did the family do?

    a. They ate breakfast
    b. They visited an onsen
    c. They rented a car
    d. They toured the city

2. Motomachi has a lot of what?

    a. Towers
    b. Hilly roads
    c. Old buildings
    d. Highways

3. While going up Hachimanzaka, what was everyone doing?

    a. Making puns
    b. Eating snacks
    c. Chatting
    d. Taking pictures

4. What sound does the onomatopoeia 「カシャカシャ」 represent?

    a. Water dripping
    b. Rolling
    c. Clicking
    d. Money

5. What is the translation of "uncool" or "lame"?
   a. ださい
   b. よい
   c. さむい
   d. ひろい

6. 「うっさい」is a more colloquial way to say which word?
   a. ださい
   b. うまい
   c. うるさい
   d. うるざい

7. Fill in the blank to complete the sentence:
   A: このシャツは格好いいと思う？（こんしゃつはかっこういいとおもう？）
   B: ううん、ちょっと＿＿＿。
   a. よい
   b. ださい
   c. ひろい
   d. さむい

8. Fill in the blank to complete the sentence.
   A: 助けて、助けて、助けて。。。！
   B: ＿＿＿！
   a. すっぱい
   b. たかい
   c. ださい
   d. うるさい

9. What was Akemi impressed by?

    a. The height of the hill
    b. The scenery
    c. The lack of litter on the ground
    d. The clear ocean

10. What did Takeshi and Hitomi want?

    a. They wanted to swim in the ocean
    b. They wanted to be in a picture
    c. They wanted their mother to carry them
    d. They wanted to go home

第二十二章
函館の夜景

夜になり、小林家は函館の夜景を見るため、函館山へと向かった。函館山のロープウェイから函館の夜景が見えてきた。

明美：本当に綺麗な景色ねえ。

久：ロマンチックだなあ、明美。

玲：お父さん。またあ?やだ、はずい。

アレックス：あっちが、さっき行った元町ですかね?

明美：アレックスって方向音痴ね。

玲：アレックス は方向音痴かもしれないけど、直人みたいに音痴じゃないよ。

直人：オレ、音痴じゃないけど!

明美&久：クスクス

武（たけし）＆瞳（ひとみ）：クスクス

直人（なおと）：武（たけし）、クスクスって笑（わら）ってんじゃねーよ！

語彙（ごい）

夜景（やけい） night view

見（み）るため in order to see

ロマンチック romantic

方向音痴（ほうこうおんち） a person with no sense of direction

笑（わら）ってんじゃねー don't laugh

QUIZ
DAY 22

1. Why did the Kobayashi's go to Mount Hakodate?

    a. They wanted to hike
    b. To see the night view
    c. To visit an onsen
    d. To have dinner

2. What did the family ride while at Mount Hakodate?

    a. A trolly
    b. A bus
    c. A ropeway
    d. A segway

3. What did Hisashi think of the view?

    a. It was too dark to see
    b. There were too many people
    c. It was romantic
    d. There weren't enough trees

4. What is the Japanese translation of "yuck"?

    a. やばい
    b. やだ
    c. やっかい
    d. やぶい

5. Someone who is helpless in all matters can be called what?

   a. おんち
   b. あんた
   c. おっさん
   d. あつ

6. What is the meaning of「方向音痴」(ほうこうおんち)?

   a. A person who is a free spirit
   b. A GPS tracking system
   c. A person with no sense of direction
   d. A person who is tone-deaf

7. What onomatopoeia is used to represent the sound of giggling?

   a. グズグズ
   b. クズクズ
   c. グズグズ
   d. クスクス

8. Fill in the blank to complete the sentence:
   A: 私のペットのゴキブリに撫でてみて(わたしのぺっとのごきぶりをなでてみて)
   B: ダメダメダメ!絶対___!(ダメダメダメ!ぜったい___!)

   a. クスクス
   b. おんち
   c. やだ
   d. ほな

9. Hitomi thinks that Alex is good with directions.

    a. True
    b. False

10. What does Rei accuse Naoto of being?

    a. Hopeless
    b. A bed-wetter
    c. A bad student
    d. A troublemaker

第二十三章
サル山温泉

次の日の朝、小林家は熱帯植物園に行った。熱帯植物園ではサルが温泉に入ることで人気の観光スポットだ。

植物園の人：おはようございます。

久：おはようございます。サルが温泉に入っているところを見たいんですが。

植物園の人：サルが温泉に入るのは、冬の１２月から春の５月まで６ヶ月間なんです。８月は暑すぎますから。

久：そうなんですか？

明美：残念だけど仕方がないわね。じゃあ植物園に入園するのはやめましょう。

玲：お父さん、ネットで調べてなかったの？

久：皆、ごめん。見逃したみたい。

アレックス：お父さん、大丈夫(だいじょうぶ)です。じゃあ、これから皆(みんな)で函館港(はこだてみなと)まつりに行(い)きましょう。

語彙(ごい)

サル monkey
熱帯(ねったい) tropics
植物園(しょくぶつえん) botanical garden
人気(にんき) popular
冬(ふゆ) winter

QUIZ
DAY 23

1. Where did the Kobayashi family go in the morning?

    a. A hiking trail
    b. A zoo
    c. A museum
    d. A botanical garden

2. What is a popular tourist spot?

    a. Where the pandas play
    b. Where the monkeys enjoy the onsen
    c. Where the lions sleep
    d. Where the sea lions do tricks

3. What month is it now?

    a. December
    b. May
    c. August
    d. February

4. What is the translation of "it can't be helped" in Japanese?

    a. やっぱり
    b. ざんねんだけど
    c. しかたがない
    d. なにもない

5. When should 「〜たいんですが」 be used?

   a. When being polite
   b. When you are angry
   c. When you are sad
   d. When you are in a hurry

6. True or False: 「しかたない」 is an acceptable, shortened form of 「しかたがない」

   a. True
   b. False

7. Using 「〜たいんですが」 what would be the polite form of the verb かう (to buy)?

   a. かうたいんですが
   b. かわたいんですが
   c. かたいんですが
   d. かいたいんですが

8. Fill in the blanks to complete the sentence:

   A: パーティーに行きたいと思うけど仕事があるから行けないみたいです (ぱーてぃーにいきたいとおもうけどしごとがあるからいけないみたいです)
   B: そうっか。___ね。仕事頑張って (そうっか。___ね。しごとがんばって)
   a. よかった
   b. しかたがない
   c. ずるい
   d. おもしろい

9. True or False: The family enjoyed their time at the botanical garden.

    a. True
    b. False

10. At the end of the chapter, where is the family heading?

    a. To a festival
    b. To a zoo
    c. To a concert
    d. To their hotel

第二十四章
函館港まつり

小林家は、港まつりの会場である函館市内にいた。地元の人達は、いか踊りを踊っていた。

地元の人達：函館名物いか踊りー！いか刺し、塩辛、いかソーメン♪

もひとつおまけに、いか ポッポー！

いか、いか、いか、いか、いか踊り♪

いか、いか、いか、いか、いか踊り♪

直人＆武＆瞳：いか、いか、いか、いか、いか踊り♪

いか、いか、いか、いか、いか踊り♪

明美：皆も一緒に踊ったら？ほら、お父さん、アレックス、玲も！

玲：やだー、はずい！

明美：パパンのパン、パパンのパン。はい、背伸びして♪

　　　ケンケンして。はい、ジャンプして♪

アレックス：クラスメイトに会いたくないよね。

玲：言えてるー。

語彙

港 harbor

まつり festival

会場 meeting place, assembly hall

踊り dance

会いたくない do not want to meet

QUIZ
DAY 24

1. What were the local people doing?

    a. Riding bicycles
    b. Playing music
    c. Playing games
    d. Dancing

2. What does Akemi want to do?

    a. Ride a bike
    b. Play music
    c. Play games
    d. Dance

3. True or False: Rei likes her mother's idea.

    a. True
    b. False

4. True or False: The 〜たら verb form can be used to make suggestions.

    a. True
    b. False

5. Which of the following translates to "you said it" when you want to agree with someone?

   a. 言った
   b. 言えてる
   c. 言いました
   d. 言う

6. What is the conditional たら-form of the verb 「たべる」 (to eat)?

   a. たべったら
   b. たべるたら
   c. たべたら
   d. たべるったら

7. What is the conditional たら-form of the verb 「いう」 (to say)?

   a. いいたら
   b. いうたら
   c. いうったら
   d. いったら

8. Fill in the blanks to complete the sentence:
   A: やっぱり、温泉は最高だね！(やっぱり、おんせんはさいこうだね！)
   B: ___ね。すごく気持ち(___。すごくきもち)

   a. そうかも
   b. 言えてる
   c. どうだろう
   d. なかなかない

9. True or False: Alex sees some of his classmates.
    a. True
    b. False

10. True or False: Rei agrees with what Alex says.
    a. True
    b. False

第二十五章
屋台

小林家は、函館港のお祭りの屋台に行った。屋台には、鉄砲屋さん、金魚すくい、綿あめ、くじ引き、お面、フランクフルト、お好み焼き屋さんなどが並んでいた。

明美：どのお面にする?

武：ピカチュー がいい!

瞳：キティちゃんがいい!

直人：オレ、金魚すくいしてくる!

久：直人、待ちなさい!

アレックス：僕が行きます。

久：アレックス、悪いね!

金魚すくいのおじさん：いらっしゃい。チャンス は三回だよ。

直人：ありがとう。えい!取れないなあ、ちくしょう!えい!あー超ムズイ!

アレックス：それ、紙?水を含むとすぐ破れるから、難しそうだな。

語彙

屋台 food stall
並んでいた were lined up
待ちなさい wait
いらっしゃい welcome
取れない cannot catch

QUIZ
DAY 25

1. What did the Kobayashi family do at the festival?

    a. Went to the local onsens
    b. Performed in the parade
    c. Checked out the yatai
    d. Danced

2. What kind of noodles does Takeshi want?

    a. Pikachu
    b. Hello Kitty
    c. Anpanman
    d. Ultraman

3. How many attempts does Naoto get at the goldfish scooping game?

    a. 1
    b. 2
    c. 3
    d. 4

4. What is the shortened version of 「いらっしゃいませ」?

    a. いらっしゃい
    b. いらしゃい
    c. しゃいませ
    d. いらっしゅ

5. 「えい」translates to what?

   a. Goodbye
   b. Hey
   c. Good morning
   d. Wait

6. What is the translation of "dang it" in Japanese?

   a. ダラダラ
   b. カシャカシャ
   c. いらっしゃい
   d. ちくしょう

7. True or False: 「マズイ」is used to describe someone as skilful.

   a. True
   b. False

8. What are the Kanji characters for the word 「マズイ」?

   a. 不林い
   b. 下味い
   c. 不味い
   d. 下木い

9. How many goldfish does Naoto catch?

   a. 0
   b. 1
   c. 2
   d. 3

10. What is the scoop that Naoto is using made out of?
    a. Wood
    b. Plastic
    c. Rubber
    d. Paper

第二十六章
花火

結局、金魚を一匹も取れなかった直人は、むっつりしていた。すると、港から大きな花火が見えてきた。

[ドッカーン、ドッカーン]

直人：うわあ、スゲー!

武：え〜ん

瞳：え〜ん

玲：お母さん、武と瞳泣き出したけどー。

明美：お父さん、カバンから耳栓だして!

久：武、瞳、この耳栓を耳に入れなさい。これで大丈夫かい？

武＆瞳：うん。

明美：凄い音ねー！でも、綺麗！

アレックス：これ、写真にちゃんと写ってるのかなあ。

玲：アレックス、アメリカの研究で、展示品の写真を撮ったグループより、写真を撮らなかったグループの方が、色々と覚えていたことが分かったって。

アレックス：へえ〜。

[カシャ]

玲：つーか、おい、話聞いてないし！

語彙

花火 fireworks
結局 in the end
耳栓 ear plugs
凄い amazing
研究 research

QUIZ
DAY 26

1. True or False: Naoto, in the end, was able to catch one goldfish.

    a. True
    b. False

2. What could be seen from the harbour?

    a. Boats
    b. The mountains
    c. Fireworks
    d. A Ferris wheel

3. Why did Hitomi and Takeshi start crying?

    a. They are sleepy
    b. The fireworks are too loud
    c. The boats are moving too quickly
    d. The music from the Ferris wheel is too loud

4. What is 「スゲー」 a colloquial form of?

    a. すぎ
    b. すぐに
    c. さすが
    d. すごい

5. What is the translation of 「スゲー」?

    a. Unfortunate
    b. Incredible
    c. Inexpensive
    d. Funny

6. True or False: In colloquial Japanese, it is not common to drop particles such as が.

    a. True
    b. False

7. True or False: Both 「か」 and 「かい」 can be used at the end of a sentence to indicate one is asking a question.

    a. True
    b. False

8. Who is most likely to have said the following sentence: 元気かい？(げんきかい)?

    a. A young boy
    b. A young girl
    c. An old man
    d. This sentence is not grammatically correct

9. What does Hisashi take out of his bag?

    a. Earplugs
    b. Food
    c. Blankets
    d. Money

10. True or False: Alex listens to Rei's advice.

    a. True
    b. False

第二十七章
登別温泉

次の日の朝、小林家は函館を出て、札幌へ向かった。途中で、登別温泉に寄った。登別温泉では、地獄祭りが開催されていた。高さ6メートルの大きな山車や、鬼の恰好をした人達が歩いているので、子供達は泣き出した。

武＆瞳：え～ん、え～ん

明美：大丈夫よ、鬼さん、怖くないから。

久：地獄祭りは、登別温泉の地獄谷から地獄のふたが開いて、大王が鬼たちを引き連れて登別温泉を訪ねる、という伝説をもとにしたお祭りなんだよ。

アレックス：そうなんですね。

直人：鬼さん、こちらー、手のなる方へー♪

語彙

寄った stopped by
高さ height
恰好 appearance
泣き出した started to cry
地獄 hell

QUIZ
DAY 27

1. After leaving Hakodate, where did the Kobayashi family head to?

    a. Sapporo
    b. Tokyo
    c. Kyoto
    d. Fukuoka

2. On their way to their new destination, where did the Kobayashi family stop?

    a. A yatai
    b. A restaurant
    c. A museum
    d. An onsen

3. How big were the floats at the Hell Festival?

    a. 4 meters
    b. 5 meters
    c. 6 meters
    d. 7 meters

4. According to the lesson, what is a translation of 「そうなんですね」?

    a. How can that be
    b. I think so, too
    c. Is that so?
    d. Of course

5. In the game of tag, what is the person who is "it" referred to as?

   a. 鬼さん
   b. 男さん
   c. 鬼ちゃん
   d. 男の子

6. What is the game of tag called in Japanese?

   a. おにごっこ
   b. かくれんぼ
   c. あそび
   d. いないいないばあっ

7. What does 「ごっこ」 mean?

   a. The name of a demon
   b. Tag
   c. Playing with friends
   d. Game of make-believe

8. According to the lesson, what is a shortened form of 「そうなんですね」?

   a. そうなん
   b. そうね
   c. そうん
   d. そなんで

9. Why did the children start crying?

   a. It is too loud
   b. They are scared of the demons
   c. They are sleepy
   d. The food at the Hell Festival was too spicy

10. According to legend, why does the demon king reveal himself?

 a. To wreak havoc
 b. To play with the children
 c. To take a bride
 d. To visit the onsen

第二十八章
富良野

小林家は、登別温泉の温泉に入り、昼ご飯を食べた後、富良野を訪れた。富良野ではへそ祭りが開催されていた。地元の人達は体にペンキを塗り、お腹を出して、へそ踊りを踊っていた。中でも小さい子供達の踊りがとても可愛かった。

直人：ウケるー！

明美：直人もへそ踊り、やってみたら？武も瞳も。こうやって、へそ をくねくねさせて・・・

武 ＆瞳：ハハハハハ

玲：お母さん、また、はずい！

久：富良野は北海道の中心にあるから、北海道のへそと言われているんだ。

アレックス：だから、へそ祭りなんですね！

語彙(ごい)

訪(おとず)れた visited

へそ belly button

地元(じもと) home town

やってみたら give a try

中心(ちゅうしん) centre

QUIZ
DAY 28

1. When did the Kobayashi family go to Furano?

    a. After breakfast
    b. After lunch
    c. After dinner
    d. While on their way to Tokyo

2. What festival was going on in Furano?

    a. The Belly Button Festival
    b. The Angel Festival
    c. The Snake Festival
    d. The Crab Festival

3. What did the people of Furano paint for the festival?

    a. The streets
    b. Their floats
    c. Their homes
    d. Their bodies

4. Which word describes something as funny or amusing?

    a. ダラダラ
    b. ハラハラ
    c. ダメ
    d. ウケる

5. Which of the following translates to "belly button" in Japanese?

   a. へそ
   b. ひじ
   c. みみ
   d. ひざ

6. Which word describes something that is wriggling or twisting?

   a. ぐにゃぐにゃ
   b. くねくね
   c. ぽつぽつ
   d. ばらばら

7. True or False: くねくね is a する-verb.

   a. True
   b. False

8. Fill in the blanks to complete the sentence:
   A: ほら、水をつけたら大きくなるよ！(ほら、みずをつけたらおおきくなるよ！)
   B: へ〜＿＿！ぼくもやってみたい！(へ〜＿＿！ぼくもやってみたい！)

   a. こわい
   b. やだ
   c. ウケる
   d. ダメ

9. True or False: Children are not allowed to dance at the festival.

   a. True
   b. False

10. According to Hisashi, where is Furano located?

    a. Next to a power spot
    b. In the very middle of Japan
    c. In the centre of Hokkaido
    d. At the apex of the Earth

第二十九章
札幌

小林家は、富良野を出て、札幌に着いた。札幌でジンギスカンを食べて、大人達はサッポロビールを飲んだ後、お盆祭りに行った。お祭りでは、地元の人達が盆踊りを踊っていた。

踊っている人：あーどーした、どーしたー♪

明美：こっちの会場では、よさこい祭りがやってるみたい。

玲：うわー、かっこいいー!

アレックス：よさこいは、若い人ばかりですね。音楽もポップなんだ。

子供達とアレックスは、よさこいを夢中で見ている。

久：明美、おふくろとおやじの商売手伝って、一緒に温泉始めるか?

明美：うん。旅行中、私もずっと考えてたんだ。カフェを売って、私も仕事やめて、銭湯を温泉にしたらいいって思ってたの。

語彙

飲んだ後 after drinking
若い young
音楽 music
夢中 absorbed in

ずっと all along, for a long time

QUIZ
DAY 29

1. What did the family eat in Sapporo?
   a. Ghengis Khan
   b. Confucious
   c. Alexander the Great
   d. Attila the Hun

2. What festival did the family go to?
   a. The Obon Festival
   b. The Lantern Festival
   c. The Dragon Festival
   d. The Sushi FestivalT

3. True or False: The Yasakoi Festival has many young people.
   a. True
   b. False

4. What is a translation of 「かつこいい」?
   a. Puzzling
   b. Good-looking
   c. Strange
   d. An expected result

5. The word 「恰好」(かっこう) is used to describe what?

   a. Personality
   b. Appearance
   c. Attitude
   d. Intelligence

6. True or False: In spoken Japanese, it is common to omit the particle を.

   a. True
   b. False

7. True or False: 「かっこいい」 can only be used to describe how a person looks.

   a. True
   b. False

8. Choose the best option to fill in the blanks in the following sentence: この映画___見たことないね(このえいが___みたことないね)

   a. The sentence is correct without filling in the blank
   b. を
   c. Both a and b
   d. No option is correct

9. What kind of music is played at the Yosakoi Festival?

   a. Enka
   b. Rock
   c. Jazz
   d. Pop

10. What do Akemi and Hisashi decide to do?
    a. Start an onsen
    b. Participate in the Yosakoi Festival
    c. Buy a home in Sapporo
    d. Buy a cafe

第三十章
小林家の未来

小林家は、札幌から東京に戻ってきた。小林家では、大切な家族と友達が皆の帰りを待っていた。

クロエ：アレックス、お帰り!

アレックス：ただいま!

祖父母：皆、お帰り。

明美、久、玲、直人：ただいま。

クロ：ワン、ワン!

久：おふくろ、おやじ、俺と明美で銭湯を継いでもいいかい？

玲：えー、マジで言ってる？

明美：私が仕事をやめて、お父さんがお店を売って、銭湯を改築して・・・私達で、温泉を始めたいんです。

祖父母：本当かい？

玲：まあ、清水寺と、城崎温泉の商売繁盛のご利益を もらってきたから、きっと大丈夫じゃん！

久：玲もたまにはいい事言うじゃないか。

小林家：ハハハハハ。

（小林家の未来はこれからだ、と久は思った。）

おしまい。

語彙

戻ってきた returned, came back
大切 precious, important
お帰り welcome home

やめて quit

たまには sometimes

QUIZ
DAY 30

1. Where did the Kobayashi family go from Sapporo?

   a. Nagasaki
   b. Tokyo
   c. Hokkaido
   d. Furano

2. Who was waiting for the Kobayashi's to return?

   a. Alex's mother and father
   b. Supermarket customers
   c. Nobody
   d. Friends and family

3. True or False: Rei knew her parents' plan to take over her grandparents' business.

   a. True
   b. False

4. What is a standard way to greet someone who has just come home?

   a. おまたせしました！
   b. でていけ！
   c. おかえり！
   d. はじめまして！

5. In Japan, which one of the following is usually said to announce you have arrived home?

    a. ただいま!
    b. あとで!
    c. こんあいだ!
    d. もうすぐ!

6. Young people commonly use 「かい」 to indicate they are asking a question.

    a. True
    b. False

7. Which of the following is used to ask rhetorical questions?

    a. どすえ
    b. じゃないか
    c. ではありません
    d. でございます

8. What are the Kanji characters for 「ただいま」?

    a. 只今
    b. 口今
    c. 只琴
    d. 匹琴

9. True or False: Akemi is going to quit her job.

    a. True
    b. False

10. True or False: Hisashi thinks that Rei never says anything of substance.

   a. True
   b. False

おわり。

ANSWER KEY

DAY 1

1. c
2. b
3. c
4. a
5. d
6. d
7. a
8. b
9. b
10. d

DAY 2

1. b
2. a
3. d
4. a
5. c
6. d
7. b
8. a
9. b
10. c

DAY 3

1. a
2. b
3. a
4. d
5. a
6. b
7. b
8. a
9. a
10. b

DAY 4

1. d
2. c
3. b
4. d
5. a
6. a
7. c
8. d
9. b
10. d

DAY 5

1. a
2. b
3. c
4. b
5. b
6. b
7. d
8. b
9. a
10. a

DAY 6

1. c
2. b
3. b
4. a
5. b
6. d
7. b
8. c
9. c
10. d

DAY 7

1. d
2. b
3. d
4. a
5. a
6. b
7. b
8. d
9. a
10. b

DAY 8

1. b
2. b
3. d
4. b
5. b
6. d
7. a
8. a
9. c
10. c

DAY 9

1. d
2. d
3. a
4. b
5. c
6. c
7. b
8. b
9. a
10. c

DAY 10

1. a
2. d
3. b
4. c
5. c
6. b
7. c
8. d
9. b
10. d

DAY 11

1. a
2. c
3. b
4. d
5. c
6. b
7. d
8. c
9. b
10. d

DAY 12

1. a
2. c
3. b
4. a
5. b
6. c
7. b
8. a
9. a
10. b

DAY 13

1. b
2. c
3. a
4. b
5. b
6. d
7. c
8. c
9. d
10. a

DAY 14

1. b
2. a
3. d
4. b
5. d
6. b
7. a
8. c
9. a
10. b

DAY 15

1. b
2. c
3. b
4. c
5. a
6. c
7. b
8. c
9. b
10. c

DAY 16

1. d
2. a
3. c
4. d
5. b
6. d
7. b
8. d
9. d
10. b

DAY 17

1. c
2. a
3. c
4. c
5. a
6. d
7. d
8. b
9. a
10. d

DAY 18

1. a
2. a
3. b
4. a
5. b
6. c
7. b
8. a
9. d
10. c

DAY 19

1. d
2. a
3. d
4. d
5. b
6. c
7. d
8. b
9. c
10. b

DAY 20

1. b
2. c
3. a
4. c
5. b
6. c
7. c
8. b
9. c
10. b

DAY 21

1. a
2. b
3. d
4. c
5. a
6. c
7. b
8. d
9. b
10. c

DAY 22

1. b
2. c
3. c
4. b
5. a
6. c
7. d
8. c
9. b
10. a

DAY 23

1. d
2. b
3. c
4. c
5. a
6. a
7. d
8. b
9. b
10. a

DAY 24

1. d
2. d
3. b
4. a
5. b
6. c
7. d
8. b
9. b
10. a

DAY 25

1. c
2. a
3. c
4. a
5. b
6. d
7. b
8. c
9. a
10. d

DAY 26

1. b
2. c
3. b
4. d
5. b
6. b
7. a
8. c
9. a
10. b

DAY 27

1. a
2. d
3. c
4. c
5. a
6. a
7. d
8. b
9. b
10. d

DAY 28

1. b
2. a
3. d
4. d
5. a
6. b
7. a
8. c
9. b
10. c

DAY 29

1. a
2. a
3. a
4. b
5. b
6. a
7. b
8. c
9. d
10. a

DAY 30

1. b
2. d
3. b
4. c
5. a
6. b
7. b
8. a
9. a
10. b

NOTES

THANKS FOR READING!

I hope you have enjoyed this book and that your language skills have improved as a result!

A lot of hard work went into creating this book, and if you would like to support me, the best way to do so would be to leave an honest review of the book on the store where you made your purchase.

Want to get in touch? I love hearing from readers. Reach out to me any time at *olly@storylearning.com*

To your success,

Olly Richards

HAVE WE MISSED SOMETHING?

We at StoryLearning Press always take great care in creating our books and all other learning material. We pride ourselves in following rigorous procedures to ensure that you get the best possible experience from all of our material.

However, sometimes it can happen that we miss something and we need our beloved audience to help us. If you find anything that needs improvement, or you simply want to know more about the process we use in creating our material, feel free to get in touch!

Just send us an email at *feedback@storylearning.com* and we will be glad to help.

JOIN OUR 30-DAY STORYLEARNING® CHALLENGES!

StoryLearning

Did you know we run monthly online StoryLearning® challenges to help you master key aspects of Japanese?

These challenges follow the same bold principle as this book:

We take the trickiest, thorniest and most downright annoying aspects of Italian, and help you master them in 30 days flat... through the magic of StoryLearning®!

Here's what you get when you enrol:

- An exciting original story (jam-packed with examples of the language focus)
- The written story plus audio book (so you can read or listen...wherever you are!)
- Daily video lessons with an expert teacher (so you can see clearly how the language point is being used in the story)
- Daily practice exercises (to help you remember what you've learned)
- Interactive discussion and unlimited Q&A in our private membership group

We run brand-new challenges every month... so don't miss out!

Find out about this month's challenge here:

www.storylearningchallenge.com

MORE FROM OLLY

If you have enjoyed this book, you will love all the other free language learning content I publish each week on my blog and podcast: *StoryLearning*.

Blog: Study hacks and mind tools for independent language learners.

www.storylearning.com

Podcast: I answer your language learning questions twice a week on the podcast.

www.storylearning.com/itunes

YouTube: Videos, case studies, and language learning experiments.

www.youtube.com/ollyrichards

COURSES FROM OLLY RICHARDS

If you've enjoyed this book, you may be interested in Olly Richards' complete range of language courses, which employ his StoryLearning® method to help you reach fluency in your target language.

Critically acclaimed and popular among students, Olly's courses are available in multiple languages and for learners at different levels, from complete beginner to intermediate and advanced.

To find out more about these courses, follow the link below and select "Courses" from the menu bar:

www.storylearning.com/courses

"Olly's language-learning insights are right in line with the best of what we know from neuroscience and cognitive psychology about how to learn effectively. I love his work!"

Dr. Barbara Oakley,
Bestselling Author of "A Mind for Numbers"

Printed in Dunstable, United Kingdom